SAMUEL *Adams*

Our People

SPIRIT
of America®

SAMUEL *Adams*

FATHER OF THE REVOLUTION

By Ann Heinrichs

Content Adviser: Peter Drummey, Librarian, Massachusetts Historical
Society, Boston, Massachusetts

The Child's World®
Chanhassen, Minnesota

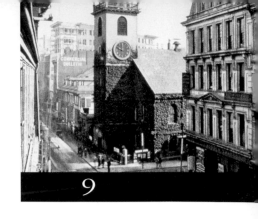

9

SAMUEL *Adams*

Published in the United States of America by The Child's World®
PO Box 326 • Chanhassen, MN 55317-0326 • 800-599-READ • www.childsworld.com

Acknowledgments
The Child's World®: Mary Berendes, Publishing Director

Editorial Directions, Inc.: E. Russell Primm, Editorial Director; Pam Rosenberg, Line Editor; Katie Marsico, Assistant Editor; Matthew Messbarger, Editorial Assistant; Susan Hindman, Copy Editor; Susan Ashley, Proofreader; Julie Zaveloff, Chris Simms, and Peter Garnham, Fact Checkers; Tim Griffin/IndexServ, Indexer; Dawn Friedman, Photo Researcher; Linda S. Koutris, Photo Selector

The Design Lab: Kathleen Petelinsek, Art Direction; Kari Thornborough, Page Production

Photo
Cover: North Wind Picture Archives; Giraudon/Art Resource, NY: 13; Corbis: 9; Bettmann/Corbis: 20, 22; Richard Cummins/Corbis: 28; Time Life Pictures/Getty Images: 11, 21; Hulton|Archive/ Getty Images: 16, 17; The Granger Collection, New York: 10, 15, 25, 26; North Wind Picture Archives: 2, 12, 18, 24; Stock Montage, Inc.: 6, 8, 14.

Library of Congress Cataloging-in-Publication Data
Heinrichs, Ann.
   Samuel Adams : father of the Revolution / by Ann Heinrichs.
      p. cm.— (Our people)
Includes index.
Contents: The man who set fires—Stirring up trouble—Father of the Revolution—A new nation takes shape.
   ISBN 1-59296-177-0 (alk. paper)
   1. Adams, Samuel, 1722–1803—Juvenile literature. 2. Politicians—United States—Biography— Juvenile literature. 3. United States. Declaration of Independence—Signers—Biography—Juvenile literature. 4. United States—History—Revolution, 1775–1783—Biography—Juvenile literature. [1. Adams, Samuel, 1722–1803. 2. Politicians. 3. United States—History—Revolution, 1775–1783.] I. Title. II. Series.
   E302.6.A2H45 2004
   973.3'092—dc22   2003018123

Contents

Chapter ONE

The Man Who Set Fires

Samuel Adams was filled with a fiery determination to be free of British rule and played an important role in shaping America as an independent nation.

"IT DOES NOT REQUIRE A MAJORITY TO PREVAIL, BUT rather an irate, tireless minority keen to set brush fires in people's minds."

These are the words of Samuel Adams. He knew a lot about setting fires. In fact, that was one of his greatest talents. But his fires were not the kind that destroy. They were the kind that create ideas and action! Adams set fires in people's minds and hearts. He did it with letters, speeches, and newspaper articles. He stirred up the American **colonists'** anger at British rule. Like a fire, this anger began as a little spark and grew to a raging blaze. From Adams's home **colony** of Massachusetts, the fires spread to other colonies. Massachusetts governor Thomas Hutchinson called Adams "the greatest incendiary [fire-setter] in the Empire."

Samuel Adams is one of America's Founding Fathers. He was not only a great writer and speaker; he was also good at organizing people and inspiring them. He didn't care if they were rich or poor. He gathered people together in meetings to fight for a common cause. He was the force behind many big events that led to the Revolutionary War (1775–1783). That's why Adams is called the Father of the Revolution.

Samuel Adams was well known in his time. Today, however, he is one of the least famous of our Founding Fathers. Other great men of his day went on to become leaders in the new United States. But once the war was over, Adams slipped into the background. He didn't mind stepping aside and letting others take over.

Samuel Adams was born on September 27, 1722. He was one of 12 children. His father, also named Samuel, owned a **brewery** and was a deacon, or minister's assistant, in Boston's Old South Church. Adams's mother, Mary Fifield Adams, was a devout religious woman. Her high moral standards guided the younger Samuel throughout his life.

The Adamses were a wealthy family. They lived in a mansion on Boston's Purchase Street, overlook-

THE ADAMS FAMILY OF MASSACHUSETTS WAS ONE OF THE LEADING FAMILIES of colonial times. Many of its members made a mark in American history. The Adams family history can be very confusing. Many Adams relatives have the same first name. See if you can follow this explanation.

Henry Adams (?–1646) was part of the original Massachusetts Adams family. He sailed from England to Massachusetts in the 1630s.

Henry's son Joseph had two sons named John and Joseph. John was the grandfather of Samuel Adams, the subject of this book. Joseph was the grandfather of John Adams (1735–1826) (below), who became the second president

of the United States. This John Adams was Samuel's second cousin. The two men sometimes worked together in helping the colonies gain independence. Both signed the Declaration of Independence.

Many more members of the Adams family became famous. President John Adams's son John Quincy Adams became the sixth U.S. president. John Quincy's son Charles Francis Adams was the U.S. minister to Great Britain. Charles Francis's son Henry Brooks Adams (1838–1918) was a historian. His best-known book is *The Education of Henry Adams.*

ing Boston Harbor. Samuel attended the Boston Latin School for eight years. At age 14, he entered Harvard College—today's Harvard University. (In Adams's time, a college was a school for high-school-age children.)

Samuel Adams graduated from Harvard College in 1740 and got his master's degree in

Adams's father served as a deacon at Old South Church (left) and hoped that young Samuel would follow in his footsteps and become a minister.

1743. Even then, the idea of revolution was brewing in the back of his mind. In a paper he wrote for his master's degree, he asked whether people had the right to oppose their leaders in order to preserve the common good. His conclusion was "yes."

After school, Adams studied law for a while. Then he went to work for a Boston merchant named Thomas Cushing. Adams was a poor businessman, though, and Cushing said he would never make it in business. Then Adams's father gave him £1,000 (1,000 British pounds) to start his own business. But Adams was terrible at managing money. He lent some of the money to a friend and lost the rest making bad business deals.

After his father died in 1748, Adams managed the family brewery. He soon lost the brewery and

Harvard College during the 1700s. Samuel Adams was not the only famous family member to attend school there—presidents John Adams and John Quincy Adams were also Harvard graduates.

much of the family fortune. In 1756, Adams became a tax collector for the city of Boston. This, too, ended in disaster. One day, his tax funds were found to be almost £8,000 short. Adams decided it was time to move on to his favorite activity—**politics!**

Interesting Fact

▶ Great Britain's American colonies used British money. Today, a British pound (£) is equal to about $1.65 in U.S. dollars.

Chapter Two

Stirring Up Trouble

SO FAR, SAMUEL ADAMS WAS NOT MUCH OF A SUCCESS in life. He didn't look like much of a leader, either. He lived in a shabby, run-down house. His clothes were often sloppy, and he sometimes drank too much. However, his life as a revolutionary leader had already begun.

A gathering of colonists protests British authority. Patriots such as Adams always took a risk in attending these meetings. If British spies overheard talk of rebellion, colonists were sometimes jailed or punished for working against the government.

Adams had made friends with many other Bostonians who opposed British rule. He wrote anti-British articles in the *Independent Advertiser,* a political newspaper. He also belonged to Boston's Caucus Club. Its members picked the candidates they wanted for public offices. Whoever they chose usually won. Little by little, Adams gathered followers from the taverns, shipyards, and streets. Soon it would be time for action.

In 1764, Britain passed the Sugar Act. It charged the colonists taxes on imports of molasses and other goods. It also put controls on the colonists' exports. Adams led the outcry against this act. He said that Parliament, Britain's lawmaking body, couldn't tax the colonists without colonial representatives in Parliament. Britain refused to allow any such representatives to be part of lawmaking. The colonists' battle cry became "No taxation without representation!"

Fighting the Seven Years' War (also known as the French and Indian War in North America) had been very expensive. King George III (left) and Parliament taxed the American colonists in an attempt to help Great Britain out of its financial difficulties.

Interesting Fact

Samuel Adams met with Boston's two rival street gangs in 1765. They were the North End gang and the South End gang. He convinced both gangs to work together with the Sons of Liberty. The gangs often took care of the more violent business of the Sons of Liberty.

Examples of tax stamps used on printed materials in 1765. The Stamp Act didn't anger the colonists because of the money it cost them—they protested because they feared further taxation without representation.

Interesting Fact

▶ The Sons of Liberty met under an old elm tree at the corner of Essex and Orange Streets. Samuel Adams called it the Liberty Tree. Effigies of hated officials were hung from its branches. British soldiers cut the tree down in 1775 and used it for firewood.

More taxes were soon to come. Britain passed the Stamp Act in 1765, which charged a tax on all printed materials. Legal documents, college diplomas, newspapers, playing cards, and even dice had to have special stamps attached to them that the colonists had to buy.

For Adams, it was time to make a move. He belonged to a secret society called the Sons of Liberty. Adams got Boston's street gangs to help them. The Sons of Liberty were real troublemakers. They held riots and burned tax stamps. They burned an **effigy** of the stampmaster and tore down tax collectors' homes. They even burned down the home of Thomas Hutchinson, the colony's **lieutenant** governor.

Adams was well-known by now. He was elected to the Massachusetts General Court in

1765. This was the colony's legislature, or lawmaking assembly. Adams's troublemaking paid off. The next year, Great Britain decided to **repeal** the Stamp Act.

In 1767, Britain passed the Townshend Acts. These ordered taxes on lead, paint, paper, glass, and tea. This was too much for Adams! In February 1768, he sent a Circular Letter to the Speakers of the House of all the other colonies. It outlined Massachusetts's position on Great Britain and taxation. A meeting to decide what

Angry colonists pull down a statue of King George III in New York. Just as British soldiers cut down the Liberty Tree for firewood, the colonists melted this lead statue of the British king to make musket balls. Records indicate that the statue produced about 42,000 bullets that were later used in the fight for American independence.

▸ John Adams, Samuel Adams's cousin, defended the British soldiers involved in the Boston Massacre at their trial. Eight had been charged with murder, but only two were found guilty.

course of action the colonies should take against Great Britain took place in September. They would write up their complaints to send to Britain's King George III. Ninety-six towns sent representatives.

While they were meeting, British warships pulled into Boston Harbor. British troops, complete with cannons, occupied the city. Adams wrote fiery newspaper articles about the soldiers' abusive behavior.

Local people, many of them members of the Sons of Liberty, heckled the troops. On March 5, 1770, some boys started throwing snowballs at British soldiers. Soon a mob of people joined in. Things quickly got out of hand, and the soldiers opened fire. When it was over, five Bostonians lay dead. This was called the Boston **Massacre.** Colonists bitterly resented this event. For Adams and his followers, it was the first battle in the fight for freedom.

Crispus Attucks is remembered for being the first to die in the Boston Massacre. In 1888, a monument was built in his honor on Boston Common.

BOSTONIANS HATED HAVING BRITISH TROOPS ON THEIR STREETS. BRITISH soldiers were called Redcoats because of their red uniform jackets. Bostonians, however, called them Lobsters and Bloody-backs.

On the evening of March 5, 1770, some boys began throwing snowballs at some Redcoats and calling them names. Soon several hundred people had gathered on King Street (now State Street). They were armed with canes, clubs, snowballs, and chunks of ice. Soldiers pushed and shoved the crowds, and finally someone shouted, "Fire!" Several Redcoats shot into the angry crowd. Three men were killed that night, and two others died later.

The next morning, a group of townspeople gathered in Faneuil Hall. They chose a committee, led by Adams, to meet with Lieutenant Governor Thomas Hutchinson. Adams demanded that Hutchinson remove the British troops from Boston. Hutchinson finally agreed, and Bostonians cheered. The common people had won!

A funeral was held for those who were killed. As many as 10,000 Bostonians marched in the procession—more than half the city's population!

Samuel Adams wrote bloody accounts of the massacre. Paul Revere printed a picture of Redcoats firing on helpless townspeople. News of the massacre spread throughout the colonies. Many colonists celebrated March 5 as a **patriots'** holiday until July 4 was declared Independence Day.

Chapter THREE

Father of the Revolution

PARLIAMENT SAW THAT IT HAD BETTER EASE UP ON the colonists to keep tempers down. In 1770, the Townshend Acts were repealed—except for the tax

Samuel Adams (left) warns a British official of the colonists' growing displeasure. Some colonial leaders were in favor of trying to work out their differences with Great Britain peacefully, but Adams was completely opposed to living under British rule.

on tea. The tea tax would be a little reminder of Parliament's authority.

Many colonists settled down after this. Without the Townshend Acts, they felt things weren't so bad after all. But not Samuel Adams! He decided that the colonists needed to communicate with one another. At a Boston town meeting in 1772, he formed a Committee of **Correspondence.** It would exchange information with other Massachusetts towns.

Soon a network of these committees sprang up all over Massachusetts. Within a few months, 80 towns had their own committees. Other colonies formed committees, too. At last, the colonists had a spirit of unity. They were learning to work together for a common cause.

Adams used the Committees of Correspondence to spread his views. At one town meeting, he delivered a report called "The Rights of the Colonists." It said that the colonists had a natural right to life, liberty, and property. They also had the right to protect and defend those things. Adams wrote that Britain was unjustly taking the colonists' rights away.

It was clear that Adams was hinting at a revolution for independence. Many of these same ideas would show up later in the Declaration of Independence. Through the Committees of Correspondence, Adams's report circulated throughout Massachusetts and the other colonies.

A VIEW OF PART OF THE TOWN OF BOSTON IN NEW ENGLAND AND BRITISH SHIPS OF WAR LANDING THEIR TROOPS

British troops land in Boston Harbor. A furious King George III ordered them to take control of the port after the colonists staged their rebellious tea party. Historians estimate that the tea lost that night was valued at about $30,000!

Great Britain passed the Tea Act in 1773. Not only did it tax imports of tea, but it also forced the colonists to buy tea from just one British trading company. Adams assembled the Sons of Liberty. On the night of December 16, 1773, they gathered at Boston Harbor. Dressed as Native Americans, they climbed aboard three British ships and dumped their cargo—342 chests of tea—overboard. Colonists called this the Boston Tea Party, but Great Britain called it a crime.

As punishment, Parliament passed a new set of laws in 1774. The colonists called them the Intolerable Acts. One law closed Boston's port. This crippled the city. It could neither receive goods nor ship out

A BOSTONIAN NAMED GEORGE HEWES TOOK PART IN THE BOSTON TEA PARTY. Here is his story of the event:

"It was now evening, and I immediately dressed myself in the costume of an Indian, equipped with a small hatchet . . . and a club, after having painted my face and hands with coal dust in the shop of a blacksmith, I repaired to Griffin's Wharf, where the ships lay that contained the tea. . . .

"We then were ordered by our commander to open the hatches and take out all the chests of tea and throw them overboard, and we immediately proceeded to execute his orders, first cutting and splitting the chests with our tomahawks, so as to thoroughly expose the tea to the effects of the water.

"In about three hours . . . we had thus broken and thrown overboard every tea chest to be found in the ship. . . .

"We then quietly retired to our several places of residence. . . ."

its own products. Other laws banned town meetings and forced colonists to house British troops.

This time, Adams used the Committees of Correspondence to spur the colonists to action. He called for a meeting among representatives of all the colonies. Again, the colonists responded. In September 1774, they called together the First Continental Congress.

Adams was pleased to see so many strong leaders there. One was Thomas Jefferson of Virginia. Another was Benjamin Franklin of Pennsylvania. Others from Massachusetts were John Hancock and Adams's cousin John Adams. Samuel Adams and

Members of the First Continental Congress met in Carpenters Hall in Philadelphia, Pennsylvania. Only 12 of the 13 colonies sent representatives to the meeting—Georgia didn't want to become involved because colonists there needed British troops to protect them from local Native American tribes.

Hancock had become good friends by this time. The Congress adopted a Declaration of Colonial Rights on October 14. It repeated many of the rights Adams had listed two years before.

The British had heard that colonists were building up military supplies for battle. On April 19, 1775, British troops marched to the Massachusetts towns of Lexington and Concord. There they faced the Minutemen. These were citizens who were ready to fight at a minute's notice. Shots rang out, and several Minutemen were killed. This event is often called "the shot heard 'round the world"—the beginning of the Revolutionary War.

The Second Continental Congress met in May 1775. Its members declared war and announced that they were free of Great Britain. Thomas Jefferson wrote a Declaration of Independence, and it was issued on July 4, 1776. However, it wouldn't be official until the congressmen signed it. In August, they met in Philadelphia. Adams stood before them and gave a speech called "American Independence."

"We have no other alternative than independence," Adams said. "Courage, then, my countrymen, our contest is not only whether we ourselves shall be free, but whether there shall be left to mankind an **asylum** on earth for civil and religious liberty." It was a stirring moment for everyone there. Taking Adams's words to heart, all 56 members signed the declaration.

Chapter FOUR

A New Nation Takes Shape

By now, the Revolutionary War was well under way. It would end in 1783 with a victory for the American colonies—the new United States! Other leaders took their places in forming the new

The Battle of Bunker Hill was fought in Massachusetts in 1775. The British narrowly won this Revolutionary War battle.

nation's government. But Samuel Adams now stepped into the background.

Adams was pleased that his own hard work had led to his goals—revolution and independence. However, he was not always happy about the way the nation was shaping up. Many important leaders were Federalists—that is, they wanted a strong central government. Adams's own second cousin, John Adams, was among them. Samuel Adams, however, believed this would be too much like the British system. He wanted the states and the people themselves to be stronger.

The new leaders met in 1787 and drew up the U.S. Constitution. It set the rules and guidelines for

The Constitutional Convention met in what is now Independence Hall in Philadelphia. George Washington (standing, far right) led the historic meeting. Samuel Adams refused to attend.

the U.S. government. Each state then had to ratify, or approve, the Constitution. Adams attended Massachusetts's ratifying convention in 1788.

As an anti-Federalist, Adams opposed the Constitution at first. He felt it did not give enough rights to individual people. He insisted on **amendments** that would guarantee those rights. The Federalists finally promised to add these amendments, so Adams was satisfied. Ten amendments, called the Bill of Rights, were added. They guaranteed

When anti-Federalists initially proposed amendments to the U.S Constitution, they had 17 changes in mind. As these changes were presented to the Senate and state leaders, however, seven were cut.

26

freedom of speech and many other rights.

George Washington, who led the colonial army, became the nation's first president. The post of vice president went to John Adams. In 1789, Samuel Adams became lieutenant governor of Massachusetts. His friend John Hancock was governor. Adams himself became governor in 1794.

Adams still disagreed with the Federalists' views. He wasn't the only one. Thomas Jefferson also favored the rights of states and individuals. Jefferson started the Democratic-Republican political party in the 1790s. That party grew into today's Democratic Party.

Adams became a Democratic-Republican and ran for presidential elector in 1796. In those days, electors from each state voted to elect the president. Whoever came in first was president, and the number-two candidate was vice president. Adams was determined to cast his electoral vote against his cousin John Adams for president. However, Samuel was defeated, and John Adams, the Federalist, became the nation's second president. Jefferson, the Democratic-Republican, became his vice president.

Tired and in poor health, Adams retired from public life in 1797. He lived to see Jefferson become the nation's third president in 1801. On October 2, 1803, Adams died at the age of 81.

Interesting Fact

▸ Today's Republican Party was born in March 1854 in Ripon, Wisconsin. It was made up of people opposed to slavery and people who wanted to settle western lands. They chose the name *Republican* in memory of Thomas Jefferson's Democratic-Republican Party.

Samuel Adams, the Father of the Revolution, had fought a good fight. Although his cousin John Adams often disagreed with him, he still admired Samuel. "Without him," John once said, "American Independence could not have been declared in 1776."

This statue of Samuel Adams stands in front of Boston's Faneuil Hall. Adams is remembered for his political service to the state of Massachusetts, as well as for his patriotism during America's battle for independence.

1722   Samuel Adams is born on September 27 in Boston, Massachusetts.

1765–1774   Adams serves in the Massachusetts legislature.

1765   Adams rallies the Sons of Liberty to protest the Stamp Act.

1767   Adams organizes colonists to protest the Townshend Acts.

1770   Five Bostonians are killed in the Boston Massacre.

1772   Adams organizes Boston's Committee of Correspondence; other towns and colonies join in the effort.

1773   Adams organizes a protest of the Tea Act, which leads to the Boston Tea Party.

1774   Adams serves in the First Continental Congress.

1775–1781   Adams serves in the Second Continental Congress.

1775–1783   The American colonies fight the Revolutionary War and win independence.

1776   Adams signs the Declaration of Independence, along with 55 other signers.

1781   Adams takes part in Massachusetts's state constitutional convention.

1788   Adams takes part in Massachusetts's convention to approve the U.S. Constitution.

1789–1793   Adams serves as lieutenant governor of Massachusetts.

1794–1797   Adams serves as governor of Massachusetts.

1803   Adams dies in Boston on October 2 at the age of 81.

amendments (uh-MEND-munts)
Amendments are changes or additions. Samuel Adams didn't want to approve the U.S. Constitution unless it included amendments to guarantee people's rights.

asylum (uh-SYE-luhm)
An asylum is a place of safety, shelter, or protection. Adams saw an independent America as the world's only asylum for individual liberties.

brewery (BROO-ur-ee)
A brewery is a factory that makes beer. Adams's father owned a brewery in Boston.

colonists (KOL-uh-nists)
Colonists are people who settle a new land for their home country and are ruled by that country. The American colonists were ruled by Great Britain.

colony (KOL-uh-nee)
A colony is a territory that is settled by people from a distant country and ruled by that country. Great Britain's 13 colonies in North America became the United States.

correspondence (kor-uh-SPON-duhns)
Correspondence is an exchange of letters or other written information. Adams started Committees of Correspondence to exchange information about British offenses and colonists' resistance activities.

effigy (EFF-uh-jee)
An effigy is a dummy or model of a real person. The Sons of Liberty hung or burned effigies of tax collectors and other British officials.

lieutenant (loo-TEN-uhnt)
A lieutenant is a public official who has the authority to act in place of someone else if needed. Adams served as lieutenant governor of Massachusetts before becoming governor.

massacre (MASS-uh-kur)
A massacre is a cruel killing of many helpless people. When British soldiers fired on Bostonians on March 5, 1770, killing several people, the event was called the Boston Massacre.

patriots (PAY-tree-uhts)
Patriots are people who love their country or homeland. Colonists who were in favor of American independence were known as patriots.

politics (PAHL-uh-tiks)
Politics is the study or practice of government. Adams's greatest interest was politics.

repeal (ri-PEEL)
To repeal is to cancel something or take it back. Great Britain's Parliament repealed the Stamp Act and the Townshend Acts because of colonists' protests.

For Further INFORMATION

Web Sites

Visit our home page for lots of links about Samuel Adams:
http://www.childsworld.com/links.html

Note to Parents, Teachers, and Librarians:
We routinely verify our Web links to make sure they're safe,
active sites—so encourage your readers to check them out!

Books

Davis, Kate. *Samuel Adams.* San Diego: Blackbirch Marketing, 2002.

Fradin, Dennis Brindell. *Samuel Adams: The Father of American Independence.*
New York: Clarion Books, 1998.

Jones, Veda Boyd. *Samuel Adams: American Patriot.* Broomall, Pa.: Chelsea
House, 2001.

Places to Visit or Contact

Boston Tea Party Ship and Museum
To learn about Adams's role in the Boston Tea Party and climb aboard a tea ship
Congress Street Bridge
Boston, MA 02210
617/338-1773

Faneuil Hall
To see where Adams attended Boston town meetings
4 South Market Street
Boston, MA 02109
617/242-5642

Index

About the Author

ANN HEINRICHS GREW UP IN FORT SMITH, ARKANSAS, AND LIVES in Chicago. She is the author of more than 100 books for children and young adults on U.S. and world history. After many years as a children's book editor, she enjoyed a successful career as an advertising copywriter. Ms. Heinrichs has traveled extensively throughout the United States, Africa, Asia, and the Middle East. She is also an award-winning martial artist.